Swimmer
in the Dust

Also by Ross Gillett

The Sea Factory, 2006

Wundawax and Other Poems, 2010

The Mirror Hurlers, 2019

Swimmer
in the Dust

Ross Gillett

PUNCHER & WATTMANN

First published in 2022
Published by Puncher and Wattmann
PO Box 279
Waratah NSW 2298

https://www.puncherandwattmann.com
web@puncherandwattmann.com

ISBN   9781922571229

Cover photo, 'Iraklion Harbour in a Dust Storm',
by Yannis Samatas with permission of explorecrete.com

Cover design by David Musgrave
Typesetting by Morgan Arnett
Printed by Lightning Source International

A catalogue record for this work is available from the National Library of Australia

For Julie, always

hats
are poems
for the head

poems
are hats
for the heart

Contents

Ash Wednesday Windows

They lay on their backs beside the dirt driveway,
waiting for walls.

They were blasted dark at the edges.
Glass sagged in the frames.

He looked down at the only views he'd ever see through them,
vistas of soil, weeds fused into the panes.

When he knelt beside one and tried the latch
I thought he was about to raise the warped sash.

But he wiped scorched dust from the powder coated metal
and stood to inspect the next burnt earth outlook.

He pointed to singed grass
pressed beneath waves of double glazing.

I left him patrolling the melted windows,
checking the shifts in perspective, the small distortions.

Missing the Rain

I think of waking her before the rain arrives,
but fatigue, that quiet storm
in her life, claims her and I surrender to it.
I know she would love the downpour

for the mercy it represents, its slant
blessing on everything – heat-threatened shrubs,
young birches, our stifling home.
But observant mercy isn't sleep.

When it comes, the rain is a shudder
in the air, a stuttering run
across the roof, and then a saving
freshness hitting everything at once.

A summer squall, a brief uproar.
I open a window in her room,
wanting the cool aftermath to reach her.
Even sleeping she is lost to exhaustion.

She wakes to find she's missed the rain.
What else can this house thrown open mean?
She walks outside to check the garden,
the world she's worried about for weeks.

She has been abandoned by her own body.
She bends to a weather-blessed mass
of flowers and foliage, then kneels.
Rain spills from the leaves onto her hands.

Kelp

These close-in breakers
are a dull swirl,
the sea weighed down
by a darkness.

They half break.
They are held back
by the life they make possible.
The gripped rock

is thick with growth,
so the ocean slows
at the last moment.
It does an anchored dance.

There's a trough
of salt foam.
A strap of kelp
surfaces and slides under.

The next swell hits.
The weed-filled wave heaves.
The weighted world
rises to the occasion.

South Coast Sonnets

We drove across the estuary,
a field of wind-stained calm, its rippled sheen
reflecting a dull acreage of sky.
Where had the mirrored clouds been
that they lived for a moment in that flattened
version of the sea, that roughed up
version of a river? We saw a battened
sail, its ribbed skin taut with a slooped
urgency. The river-imaged
sky was a helpless backdrop, a flecked plain
of tidal doubt. Would the future be staged
upstream or downstream? The sailor was again
tacking into the world's wind. The threadbare
bridge we crossed had always been there.

**

We were instant coastal addicts.
Our first wonder was a suppressed surf,
a withering offshore wind. We practised
not being blown into the sea. Just enough
leaning inland did it for us.
Next day we leaned towards the ocean
arm in arm, wind-resistant visitors
embraced by what was now an onshore
gale. Was this a marriage rite? Gestures
of spray rose from the rocks and drifted
over us. We knew the wind that blessed us
was a turncoat. We took on trust the gift
we couldn't avoid, a getaway
ocean wedding. We wore the veils of spray.

**

Call it the eternal southerly.
Breakers bloomed and faded,
ghost cliffs retreating into the sea.
An endless coastal uproar betrayed
our inland certainties. A dusk walk
took us down a slipshod path
skirting the maelstrom. We stood back
from the edge of an ocean truth,
immensity ending in collapse,
the earth-shaking landfall. Above us
clouds were turning into high-speed scraps
of themselves. We were lovers
in a gale-force world. The long gusts
wailed as they came at us.

**

We saw the surfer calling it a day,
riding in towards the undermined
bluff we stood on. No beach lay
in wait, but he casually half-planed
into shore, or what there was of it. We worried
when he disappeared from sight. Then the yellow
tip of his board came up through a hole in the scarred
platform of rock behind us. What runs below
the sea-wrecked surface of a place like this,
what do the locals know that they can rise
like bearded seals out of the ground? There's always
safe passage somewhere, but it lies
hidden. We are cave believers. Lord
we have seen the risen man with his finned board.

**

A dedicated ocean spent
years laying down the small laws
of sand. Edges of the continent
disintegrated into loose shores,
gold beneath our feet. The beaches
harboured us. Even with bad weather
beating at their doors, they were stretches
of close comfort. Our footprints receded together,
a stitched wake trailing behind us.
Weightless strands of foam crawled
after each other. In the end, the wind turned us
home through the dunes, but we were a told
story by then, our staggering narrative written
step by step across the sea's terrain.

The Insomniacs

for Amy

The small hours
are huge.

As a child
sometimes my room was miles long
when I turned on the light.

I switched it off and lay there
knowing the dark contained those distances.

Tonight
it's my sleepless daughter
who finds how far it is down a darkened hallway
to her parents' bedroom
and knocks so softly
she almost doesn't touch the door at all.

I take her back and tuck her in.

Now it's both of us
lying awake in the enormous dark,
pinning our hopes
on dawn.

All that light
hauling itself up by the bootstraps.

This Me-Shaped Home

There are times when it's locked against me.
All I feel
is an after-hours darkness.

I camp on my own doorstep
and wait for my body to swing open.

Unlock, I think.
Be a door for me to walk through into myself.

*

Sometimes I sleepwalk my way in.
I wake
to find I'm in in the strange house of my body.

Look, an attic
with so much dust on so much treasure.

Living rooms,
the walls plumbed with blood.

I am clad in flesh, the miracle material.

It all fits me
as if it is me.

*

With my lover
I can be at home
in my body.

There's a hearth
somewhere around the heart.

A threshold
that seems to be everywhere.

*

The mind
leans out of the body.

It can see almost to the end of everything.

It doesn't care
if far below
there's the muffled smashing of a window.

It's only me
breaking in.

Trajectory

after the composition 'In a Close Orbit' by Anthony Lyons

Listen as though the music were your life.
Wrestle with the tempo. Take to heart
the beautifully complicated triumph
afforded you before it falls apart.
Indeed, disintegration's in the air
the moment certainty abandons you.
After that it's how to hold together
the strangely fading world you're trekking through.
Each advance is underscored by doubt.
A pause has all the weight of a crescendo.
And so the slowing down, the thinning out,
intensities adrift somewhere behind you.
Soon you'll hear the endless silence sing.
The last chord remembers everything.

Complaint

Put the universe away for now.
I've had it up to here with its slow crawl
across the sky each night, the same old show
blazing away for aeons, wall to wall.
Our galaxy's a vague stretch of river,
a smudge of glitter backed by nothing much
except the darkness that goes on forever.
Not a bit of it that we can touch.
Closer to home the badly beaten moon
staggers around and takes its usual dive.
I'm sick of Venus wanting us to swoon
and Jupiter dining out on sheer size.
Both of them are trying to be stars.
I think that little pinkish thing is Mars.

Lunar Eclipse

My mother's face was the moon.
My father shone
his flashlight on the earth.

He was the sun.
Earth was a beach ball
propped on the kitchen table.

My father prowled.
The shadow of the world
slid across my mother.

I nodded.
I almost understood.
They let me stay up

for the real thing,
shade spilling over
the moth-eaten moon,

but I wasn't impressed.
I wanted the eclipse
my parents made,

my mother's face halved,
my father
dark behind the light.

Thumb Poem

my father's hands placed against each other
moved so the top of a thumb broke free
then sprang back into place again
the join covered by his big finger

the effort he put into it was wondrous
the slight grunt and the gritted teeth
as he tugged at the stubborn thumb
which was putting up a fight

I loved the halved thumb
springing apart and back together
and my father actually smiled in the end
doing this terrible thing to himself just for me

The Game

When they rush past like sudden apparitions
and tear aside the curtain of the air

screaming at each other You're dead You're dead,
ignoring us as if we've never lived

we do the right thing, like obliging ghosts.
We stand aside and let them carve their path

our grown-up talk suspended in mid-sentence,
everything on hold until we've seen the last

and smallest child come charging after them,
lagging behind but still a part of it

almost falling as she's pulled along
by the strong invisible rope of the game.

Making a Meal of It

*"The **border with Victoria** will remain closed…"*
*Annastacia Palaszczuk, Premier of **Queensland**, June 29, 2020*

Victoria, what have you done with New South Wales?
Have you swallowed the oldest state? Eaten
all that outback, devoured the Darling?
Our shrivelled rivers won't know themselves
so far north, swollen with redneck rain.

Melbourne, with your monstrous hotspots,
lockdown fever and cancelled comedy
– so much infectious humour – you have licked
the city of the fancy coves, the Harbour
and the Coat Hanger, clean off the map.

Your dull bay and boring grid have won.
You can wave goodbye to a civic envy
fed by your lack of glamour. My city,
you have gone viral, you have led
a hungry Garden State to victory.

And Melbourne, stifle predictable guilt.
We know how your wintry sensitivity
gets in the way. Your Waistcoat Bridge
is triumphant. Don't let the Opera House
stick like a wishbone in your throat.

Danger Bay

There's a lovely lacework of salt
between your shoulder blades

a skin of sand
on your arms

and we own this steep beach.
There's no one for miles

not even a ship
peering over the walls of the sea.

Waking to Rain

Rain is stitching us up,
working away at the tin roof
with its millions of needles.

It is sewing threads of winter
into our sleep.

*

We are betraying sleep.
We have switched our allegiance to the rain.

Woken by the command
of a downpour,
we lie together under the weight of the rain.

*

When we sleep again
we will have rain on our minds.

There will be the two of us
with our deluge-driven dreams.

Everything will be a marriage of rain and sleep.

Ascending from the Wreck

Leave the rich disaster
where it rests. Follow
the balloons of your spent breath
to the surface. They are pebbles
of light. They want the world.

To be alone with a lost
radiance, an ancient wealth
– now there's a death.
Treasure, that sweetener
of dreams. Keep surfacing.

Break through to the ocean
of air, its people who insist
on needing you, on being needed.
Let the sunken vessel lie
sprawled and split.

You will remember
the marine season, the spillage
of drowned beautiful things,
but life will be necessary now.
Someone will take you in.

There will be a winter home
guarded by young birch trees.
There will be dark days, then a day
of the smallest possible leaves,
the tiny beginnings of shade.

The sky is inhabited
by a saving light. Someone
has harboured you, give
yourself as shelter in return.
Let the sea breed its wreckage.

Walls

for Paul Morton

There was a dark blue wall
so high and long
he thought a building stood beside the wharf.

But when he leaned back and looked up
he saw it was the ship.
It took him to another country.

He was ten years old
and like all of us
he has had to deal with walls since then.

We suffer the small imprisonments of living.
Freedom
is always on the other side of everything.

But he learned early
that walls don't have to be climbed.
When walls are high

and seem to lean over you,
they might be ships.
A wall can sail away and take you with it.

The Wall

We came down from the betrayed terraces
to the sea wall. Its solid presence
reassured us. Beachside paddocks
flourished, their pasture seasoned by spray
knocked loose from the breakers.

Hunched in our overcoats, we trekked
beside the wind-tilted fences,
down the pale road through dunes
barely kept at bay by buried mesh.
Houses were waist deep in sand.

We knew this wasn't permanence.
Time engulfed us, but the wall
stood for something, and even its bulk
flinched. Not that it offered hope
of a home. It was all barrier.

It has stayed like this. Our dwellings
crouch in the dunes. The years,
whatever they are, blow over us.
We have driftwood tables, doorways
always in need of sweeping.

And the future, whatever that is,
still clings to the horizon.
We have a shaken faith in it. Each day
we wake to a world scoured clean
of dreams. We check the wall.

Paling Fence

See how it's gone grey with age.
The frail palings put up with so much.

Think of that timber twister the rain
or the nail-loosening gales of winter.

Even a good summer threatens the fence.
All that heat on its thin flanks.

Almost unnoticeably it begins to fray
as if letting go its life as a barrier.

Splits and slippages become part of it.
No wonder it begins to let the light through.

There are splinters of brightness
where the fragile overlapping fails.

Whatever space is on the other side
seems to be giving off a radiance.

This opening up can be the fence's death
as the whole fabric starts to fall apart.

Soon the seasonal work of straightening,
fixing and replacing should begin.

For now, there's something about the way
flaws in the fence intensify the light

from the overgrown land next door.
The palings are a threadbare darkness

and the neighbouring unseen undergrowth
makes itself known in slivers of glare.

If weathering betrays the fence like this,
hinting at a blaze of light behind it,

think of what disintegration means.
Rails dislodged, whole palings gone,

light unleashed across the boundary.
Imagine the incandescence of collapse.

Language

1

Language is
loaves and fishes.
There are millions of us
hungry for new meaning
and only so many sounds, only so many symbols.
Strange that there's always more than enough
revelation to go around.

2

If I take off my glasses
and lean back in my chair,
the words on the screen merge into an interesting blur,
strata of grey illegibility,
a coastline of possible meanings.
And there, persisting in the middle of it all, the cursor
flashing like a heartbeat.

3

Words
interrogate each other.
And they use some muscle.
Words love nothing more than leaning on other words.
They are sometimes seen using undue force.
They twist each other's meanings.
But all of them stay mute.
The lips of words are buttoned.
They never squeal.

Remembering Iraklion

The ship's wake
simmered down as it fanned out.

We were letting everything slip away behind us.
Cities, islands, other lovers.

*

Our destination came alongside at sunrise.
It was shedding darkness
from rooftops and roads.

When the ferry stopped its shuddering
Iraklion bumped against us.

*

We almost had the dawn streets
to our long-shadowed selves.

There was a man
pushing his broom with a sly lightness of touch.

He seemed half asleep
but he gave us a wink,
a blessing almost too quick to catch.

*

In Lion Square
our rucksacks leaned together
on a stone step,
two battered canvas torsos.

My fellow traveller,
all faded blue jeans and fierce blue eyes,
stood guard as I scouted for rooms.

Fountain beasts watched over her,
lions carved by someone who had never seen a lion.
Never-ending streams of water
flowed from their open mouths.

An image of eternity.
A poor substitute for a roar.

*

The door of one hotel was not quite closed.
I took that narrow strip of darkness at its word.

The reception desk
was a tourist altar.
Plaster saint,
pen and register on chains
and a bell.

The deity appeared feet-first
down steep stairs.
He wore tight robes –
a fisherman's jumper and suit trousers
pulled on over pyjamas.

*

The staircase was the twisted
eye of a needle,
a stretched gate.

We squeezed through
into a dingy rented heaven
with a view of the harbour of Heracles.

*

From our one window
we could see the ship cranes dip and swing.

We were safe
from all that departure,
all that arrival.

*

That night, the dust storm,
an airborne desert coming for Iraklion.
Grains of the Sahara piled up on the windowsill.

In the morning our harbour outlook
was lost in a parched mist.

*

We saw a dimmed greatness.
An arid glory
draped the city in its veils.

Our refuge from the withering storm
was a crooked room
and a mattress so old and soft
lying down was falling into one another.

We left Iraklion to its faded fate.

*

The dust was with us in the Cretan streets,
a gritty benediction.

My lover waved to me
from the end of a clouded street
in the faintly invaded city.

She beckoned with both arms.
She was a swimmer in the dust.

*

What sort of truth was it,
that vagueness at the window?

Something vast was in the air.

The sky was a dull glow at the end of every street.
We walked the breakwater
and saw an earth-coloured surf.

*

In my dream
the lions are coming home.
A fountain follows them and turns into more lions.

We are both there
waiting for lions.

*

When the wind had nothing more to give
and the miracle of the dust ended,
we drove to a treeless beach.

It was a day for distances.

The sea was a flat enormous presence
drawing a line under the sky.
The afternoon went for miles in all directions.

We lay on the forgiving sand
and slipped into each other's lives.

*

The rain remembered Iraklion.

It sloped in from the west
and a darkness
gleamed in the streets.

From the breakwater
we saw the dust going to sea.

We stared into a flowering tide.

*

These streets, these memories
– as if there's a way through
the haze of time.

In the blink of an eye
we were swept up
and emptied into each other's arms.

The god of small hotels
grudged us a key.

The harbour signalled
while a room embraced us.

A beach became an anchorage.

*

It was all a strangeness
breeding certainties between us.

Even the dust
was a way of seeing.

*

Iraklion
we kept the key.

Daedalus and Son

If you'd survived the sky, if you'd held on to a wing
and landed feet first, you could have scrambled

a makeshift swim. Even a few feathers may have helped,
fistfuls of buoyancy, remnants of flight doing their duty.

The proverbial mermaid might have swerved out of a wave
and saved you. But you fell headlong and empty handed.

We were meant to vanish into air, lose ourselves
in the territories of cloud. Home was a dark horizon line

when you veered upwards, a diver going against the grain
of gravity. I lost you in a pool of blinding light

and you washed up on the wrong coast, a blotched doll.
I've made my burnt beach offering to the sea god

and his accomplice the sun. The fatted calf is brine-soaked
ash. It's really for you, my flier, my obliterated boy.

*

Maze maker, father, I'm fine, here on the foggy borders
of oblivion. I'm still your heat seeker, I can smell summer

way out there in the fields of time – I remember time.
So I have to tell you: I touched the sun, its seething life.

My body flared with a sacred blaze, and your handiwork
fell apart only then. The freedom you invented for me

lasted longer than it should have, frail and almost weightless
as it was. I forgive the provocation of your warning,

forgive me my sunstruck hopes. I wanted to bring you
sky stories, I wanted to see the edge of the world,

but unthinkable heat and the sea's intensity greeted me.
No mermaid surfaced, no sea-cold hand held mine

as I went under. It's possible to burn and drown
in the one instant. Whatever surrounds me, it isn't distance.

*

Your mother stirs in her sleep and mutters some song.
It's her dream swim. She sings your name as she saves you.

We should have flown by night – the innocent glitter of stars,
a touchable moon, the home shore conspicuous

in that cool glow. I'd have risked dew on the feathers.
I've ditched the wings. I wish the thread I handed Ariadne

had stitched the hem of her wedding dress, and the king
had abandoned my labyrinth plan. I couldn't regret

freedom we never needed. By day, your mother still sings
as she builds you a shrine of sun-baked salt, and the sea wind

makes landfall on the beach. I imagine you riding it in,
tilting your wings and leaning back as you descend.

I walk the sloped wet sand, watching each gust shimmer
across a skin of water. Wing prints touching down.

*

Never regret our breakout flight. My world is a damp haze.
A directionless wind tugs at everything, so grant me

the remembered ecstasy of disaster — the way your wings
hauled me higher and higher, hot thin air around the sun,

then a radiance that took my breath away. The fall
was a last twisted minute of living. If I ever come home

I'll be wingless, trudging over the dunes, a footsore ghost
knocking at the back door. Tell my mother not to wait up.

I hope she keeps my salt shrine safe from the king tides.
As for you, my wing builder, my escapee, my father,

leave your beach to the breakers, their saltwater hedges,
their foam seedlings, the endless harvest of sand.

I'll never fly in, I'll never swoop down. I'm grounded.
They've given me my earthbound shroud, my stone sky.

from The Atlantis Diaries

last night
a new lover

she pulled her stockings on
and my heart laddered

she left me with the salt taste
of skin

a lick
of love

*

she turned on her heel
stepped under

the shambling fence
of a breaker

and walked off
down the lanes of the sea

the green walls
ate her up

*

drunk
in Atlantis

I snatch a bottle
out of the dark air

and drink its message
unread

*

I step outside
put my foot down

and a wave
heads up the silt street

a rippling
that never looks back

as it vanishes into the jade alleys
the swaying rooms

still hunting
as it fades

*

after dark
when the tide blows in through the windows

lovers stir in their sleep
and throw their stone arms around each other

they scrape
through the night

To the Lifeguard

for Nathan Curnow

"Blessed are the poor swimmers
for they shall be saved."
(The Beatitudes of St Adjutor)

If I fall in
dive after me.

*

Diving's a way of falling.

*

I've seen you walk on water.
Up to my eyes in chlorine blue
I watched you stroll across the turbulence.
You were patrolling the pool's edge
but from where I floundered
you were the miracle man
with your butterfly shoulders
and that look that sees everything.

*

Shovers and duckers
girl pinchers
big kids tugging little kids under,
beware.

You are known
by your bleached hair and dark hearts.

Lifeguard,
send them away slouching and dripping.
May this fake lake
be a place of peace.

*

Keep your expert eye on us
as we half walk half float around each other
or tread water in the deep end,
putting so much effort into going nowhere.

*

Struggling with our national stroke
I crawl through the small waves,
turning my face to one side.
My open mouth trawls for air.
I'm an amphibious sideshow clown
moving through the water.

*

Maybe the breast stroke is best.
The hands form a prow,
a gesture of prayer
before they push the water away.
Swimming is praying.
Lifeguard, hear my prayers.
Save me from my sinkable self.

*

You are a wavery tall person standing over me.
You come apart at the seams and join up
with every wobble of the water.

*

I'm the hopeless swimmer,
the underwater wanderer,
the pool bottom drifter.
See me and I'm saved.

Love Song

after Miroslav Holub's "Fairy Tale"

I think the unending rain
is with us tonight

there's weather
at the window

a slant roar
on the roof

it's time to rise
and enter the rain

let's fold up our closeness
and take it with us

we'll need its warmth
for the journey

we'll be walking through walls
of rain

and if you ask me
where is the world

I'll say this
is the world

this fallen
shimmer

this rain
that has woken us at last

Mild Climate Snow

Something tumbles out of a strange sky
and turns to nothing as it goes to ground,
but how its cold clear camouflage is found
as it floats in, and what it is, and why
it falls on such a slant with such a sly
silence, an avalanche of withheld sound,
and why the fences and the trees aren't crowned
by all this ragged whiteness drifting by
– well, an act of disappearance swarms
down on this temperate world, things fade
as they arrive, no need for questions, blend
into the ground you're on, the quiet storms
of presence persist, everything is made
instant and endless run-off in the end.

Rain Sonnet

Rain swings past the corner of the house,
gust after gust roaming in like blurred
versions of a house, structures loosened,
shifting and adrift, roof beams straying
on the run, walls and shapeless rooms
unfolding into what is purely rain.

From where I am, standing in the lee
of my grey home, it seems that maybe all
houses are cousins of the rain, and we,
weathered inhabitants, live in a loose
relationship with it, and might be
rain at heart, as untranslatable
and loosely put together as we are,
like this day's downpour, like a life of rain.

Bringing on the Rain

You were asleep, and as I braced the door
for quietness, pulling against the push
to open it, the well-timed rain arrived,
a soft roar sweeping in along the roof
and drowning any sound I might have made.

Coincidence – though why not have the weather
attentive to our house and the dark room
with you asleep in it, and the rain held
in readiness, standing by until
my wanting not to wake you called it in.

Impossible as you may think that is,
it's all I have by way of holding to
the darkness, and the lateness of the hour,
and how my coming in to sleep beside you
hauled the rain across our lives that night.

Better Weather

The children of the sky are coming home,
bringing warmth all twisted up
in their blue beach towels.
They trail them through the trees.

They've been away for weeks.
They've been out there hunting the sun.
Now they are daubing the walls
and fences of the world

with light. They are getting us up,
dragging us from dreams
of going nowhere on the grey
directionless gale of sleep.

We wake to the real
truant wind at our door,
the flash of leaves, the squeak
of sneakers on the skylights of our life.

The Unknown Wonders

The Guard
Lovers, there's a locked door between us
but I'm on your side. You are about to be
bereft of darkness. Its hold on you
has been loosened by the dawn.

If the day stumbles upon your secret
you are doomed. I'm your mystery keeper
and you are the confirmed rumour
I've sworn to defend from disclosure.

Remain a hidden truth, be unknown
wonders. Now is the time to embrace
separation. In these stone rooms
the windows are turning pale with dread.

The Knight
Lady, are we ghosts, that dawn is our enemy?
Sometimes it's hard to believe in our bodies,
these phantoms of flesh, these weightless
selves we become in one another's arms.

I can vanish through you at the first kiss
but now with this intrusion of light
it seems I'm all too solid evidence.
I could have us slain simply by being seen.

My slender deceptive hope, put on
your waiting clothes. The world is given
to the close-hearted. May daylight also
be a veil. The dawn is swarming over us.

The Lady
I'm no ghost, but think of me as your poltergeist
if you like. I'm your rogue spirit, creating
havoc in the great room of your heart.
Dawn won't shake you free of this wraith.

Admit it, we are fleshed entities. We haunt
one another at close range, we cannot tell
whose skin is whose. If the day tears us apart
it will have our beautiful wreckage on its hands.

My darkness man, I wish we could bury the sun,
that waste of radiance. Absence is all we have
as an answer. Look, the first slivers of light
have forced their way in. Kiss me and disappear.

Night Beach

This is the weather-beaten territory
of your story,
the legend I live with.

So many tough curves of coast
in the sea's mind,
but tonight this slender beach

with its line of dunes on the edge of breakthrough
seems like an afterthought.
We can all be betrayed by the truth.

*

It's the seascape
of memory.
The beach with its sluiced perfection

soft underfoot,
the dunes in their small-hour darkness
looming like stationary breakers,

an almost invisible ocean.
The past rolling in with a roar
of arrival.

*

He's my shadow,
my second-guesser.
Distant and dismissed as he is,

there are beached days
when he's always a heartbeat ahead of me.
I touch you and he outreaches me

by a fingertip.
When I kiss you
he wins by the skin of his teeth.

*

Bronzed by dawn,
staggered headlands flank the bay.
Everything between them thunders and drifts.

Who could trust the sea in this breaking light?
Even the dunes
have their faint stinging song.

The mind is a dark beach.
I can feel the shifting of the ocean's feet,
rumours from the other end of the world.

Onshore

Coastal sounds loosen, and the moon
is on a long shuddering run through cloud.
So much drift and drag in everything.

No point in waking you for this, you're moored
in an inlet of sleep. Your days
veer in upon themselves and disappear.

You speak of half-remembered dreams, forgotten
fresh starts, the maze of endings. A damaged
oblivion keeps dissolving into dawn.

Tonight the wind has brought the ocean closer,
shepherding its dense roar inland.
Our garden's crowded with the sound of breakers.

You yearn for weightlessness. I tell you
we're dwelling in it. Beach mist climbs the dunes,
wanders the neighbourhood and settles in.

We live with spindrift stranded in the streets
and rumours of the sea in every room.
Time hardly knows it has us on its hands.

Long Weekend

When you call from the coast
I can feel a tidal pull.
Your voice is edged with a blur

of beach sound,
the slurred words of the sea.
I imagine you knee deep,

breakers behind you,
the backwash pulling
at your stance.

Everything you tell me
has an undertow of meaning.
Whatever I say

is dragged off course.
When you call next time
keep the ocean out of it.

Thunder Only Happens

from a line by Stevie Nicks

After a lengthy disengagement
I have married departure.

I fell in love
with oil slick rainbows.
I hankered for the two white lines
painted down the middle of the bitumen,
ribbons on the long black limousine
of the highway.

A storm found me
and I've driven into it.
The clouds are flinching with heat and light.

I've taken leave
of your senses.

> *Wherever you are*
> *the thunder*
> *gets under my skin.*

> *The horizon mumbles.*

> *We're connected by this weather.*
> *If I haul in the sky*
> *I'll find you hanging on to it.*

> *Before you went*
> *I wanted you back.*

When the double lines remind me of their satin sisters
tied to the bonnet of a wedding car
I overtake.

On wet days
there are trucks towing their own storms.
The thump of the wipers
gets me through.

The road is an endless threshold.
Speed carries me over it.

I'm a moving target.
Miss me
if you will.

> *You're somewhere*
> *in another state.*

> *The intervening sky is useless.*
> *No thought*
> *of a squall,*
> *not a hint of thunder.*

> *I need a downpour*
> *at the end of my street.*
> *I want you to be driving*
> *and your wipers*
> *harvesting rain.*

> *You've taken back your promise*
> *so keep it.*

If a roadhouse
can be a bridesmaid
I'm married.

I'm wedded
to territory.
I've booked in
to a honeymoon motel
with surround sound solitude.

Think of this as the end
of weather.

I've disowned
my half of the sky.

Great lines can be lies.

I've always said
if you're coming back
don't go
and rainless thunder
is the oldest broken promise.

Lightning is the answer
coming a split second before the question.

You are at my door.
You are about to ask for shelter
from the non-existent rain.

The sky
can hear its own heart beating.

Directions

Look into the rain.
Inside it
there is more rain.

Don't be surprised by the downpour
happening inside the downpour.

Go for a walk in it,
the rain
inside the rain.

Aubade for the Things Not Done

My cousin saw Creation
receding in a dream. He's dying
and sent me his psalm of obliteration.
I should storm the keyboard. I was crying

in defiance for him, but I haven't replied.
And my parents' ashes are unscattered.
They wait in their foot-long boxes side by side
on a shelf. He read me to sleep, she plaited

my school hair. The promises I make I keep
on hold. All my intentions are stalled.
Cousin, your vision made me weep,
Mother, Father, I called

like a lost daughter, but you'll never send
for me again. Can the past forgive?
Everything's an answer in the end.
It's dawn, the world's beginning to live

its urgent life. Miles above me, a jet
drags its bit of thunder through the sky.
That lagging roar…one day I'll get
ahead of myself. Who will I be, and why

does the unimaginable future seem
real for a moment? There must be wings
in the mind, as if my trapped intentions stream
forward into new time. Everything sings

of release, imprisoned ashes fly
from the hand. Nothing's beyond the scope
of unleashed words, those small freedoms we live by.
Cousin, I'm collapsing into hope.

The World Burglars

We break in
and start stealing air.

Our bodies
take all the space they need.

Our mouths are caves.
We fill them with consumables.

We join the language gang
and hoard words.

Our minds are hideaways
stacked with thought.

We get more and more
inside knowledge.

Soon we have designs on the future.
We want it to belong to us.

Our lives become a smash grab
for happiness.

Some of us steal hearts
and become persons of interest.

Each pilfered minute
is gold.

If we could
we'd take all the time in the world.

The Mountain Poem

Lord
we are approaching the mountain poem

when we swarmed over the first high passes
its summit was a distant sign

now we lean back
to watch its banners of cloud
fade and renew themselves

the poem is manufacturing sky

it is a great poem
flanks of forest and rock surround us
it won't let us pass

if there's no way over
there must be a way through
we want to be inside the mountain poem

and we are
it has reached for us and dragged us in

we grow close to each other
in the darkness of the poem

we may never get out
we may never know what lies beyond the poem

but we have seen its granite bones
the glimmer of its inner life
grains of luminescence

Lord
if we make it through
we will carry the smallest torches
seeds of seeing
grown in the heart of the poem

if we find the way out
we will stand on the other side of it
and remember its immensity

ahead of us will be a world without the poem

a sky
full of the best intentions

and the earth
the unfulfilled earth
thinking about the poem

Cloud Climbing

Grab the lightest line you have,
a thread
of nothing.

Throw it at the clouds.

It may take years
but one day you'll do it,
snag the edge
of a drifting cliff.

By then you will be very old,
paper thin,
weightless.

Haul yourself up.

Acknowledgements

Poems in this collection have been published by the following journals and websites: Australian Book Review, Quadrant, Antipodes, Australian Poetry Journal, Poetry Monash, Melbourne Poets Union website, *This House, My Body* (a chapbook published as part of the multi-media arts project of the same name run in the Newstead Railway Arts Hub in 2018), Newcastle Poetry Prize Anthologies 2019 and 2020, Heidelberg International City of Literature "Tagelied" Project website, Melbourne City of Literature Poet Laureates website and anthology, *Pure Poetry Recital*, a collection of poems written for the project of the same name (Art Gallery of Ballarat, 2011) and the anthology of the 2021 ACU Poetry Prize. The final poem in the collection has been accepted for an anthology of poems translated into Esperanto, to be edited by Kit Kelen.

"Paling Fence" was awarded second prize and "Ascending from the Wreck" was highly commended in the 2018 Melbourne Poets Union International Poetry Prize. "Daedalus and Son" and "Thunder Only Happens" were shortlisted for the 2019 Newcastle Poetry Prize and "Remembering Iraklion" was shortlisted for the 2020 Newcastle Poetry Prize. "South Coast Sonnets" was shortlisted for the 2020 Peter Porter Poetry Prize. "Aubade for the Things Not Done" was shortlisted for the 2021 ACU Poetry Prize. "Onshore" was shortlisted for the 2021 Bridport Poetry Prize.

In terms of people to whom I owe my thanks, and to begin at the beginning, the cover, I thank Yannis Samatas and explorecrete.com for the terrific photo of Iraklion Harbour in a dust storm, which matches perfectly the title of the book and the poem from which it is taken, "Remembering Iraklion". My gratitude goes to David Musgrave and the Puncher & Wattmann team for publishing this book, and for being such a force for good in the strange world of poems and poets. Thanks also to those others who in recent years, and in some cases for much longer, have shared the poetry experience with me in so many different ways. There is a small host of people, many of whom are fellow poets, who have provided valuable input to my work: Nathan Curnow, Ross Donlon, David Frances, Anne Gleeson, Debi Hamilton, Mary Jones, Lorraine McGuigan, Sam Morley, Richard Perry and Gudrun Markowsky, and Bruce Oakman and Barbara Coish. The Daylesford Neighbourhood Centre Poetry Group has been inspiring and entertaining me on an almost weekly basis for nearly four years, and I thank members present and past, new and old: James Baillie, Nada Celeste, Gael Elliott, Andrew Flett, Jennie Fraine, Margret Lockwood, Ros Marsden, Di Parsons, Tom Perfect, Steph Powell, Lal Von Steensen, Anne E Stewart and Bill Wootton.

To have discovered close to home a friend and writer of the calibre of John Scott is a piece of good fortune for which I thank the poetry gods. Paul Morton's deep interest in and knowledge of poetry are unique amongst those of my friends who are not themselves poets. Andrew Flett keeps drawing on his amazingly wide and deep reading to introduce me to new poems and new thoughts. It would be difficult to overstate the extent to which Paul Mason's art, his wonderful paintings and drawings, and our conversations about art and poetry, are an ongoing inspiration. Finally, love and gratitude to my wife, Julie Phillips, for her readiness to be involved in the redrafting of my poems and my life.

Notes

"This Me-Shaped Home"

This poem was written for the 'This House, my Body' arts project, Newstead Railway Arts Hub, September 2018.

"Trajectory"

A performance of 'In Close Orbit' can be found at https://www.purepoetryproject.com.au/gallery

"Making a Meal of It"

This poem was commissioned by the Melbourne City of Literature Poet Laureates project, which ran for much of 2020 during the city's lockdown and involved a different poet each week producing a poem that in some way reflected Melbourne's experience of that time. The last line of "Making a Meal of It" echoes a line in Robert Lowell's poem "For the Union Dead".

"Remembering Iraklion"

This poem was inspired by Ted Hughes' great poem, "Remembering Teheran".

"The Unknown Wonders"

This sequence of poems was commissioned by the Melbourne UNESCO City of Literature Office as part of a contribution (by six Australian poets) to the 2020 Tagelied Project run by the Heidelberg UNESCO City of Literature Office. The legend of the Tagelied – the Day (or Dawn) Song – is a mediaeval story of two lovers, a lady-in-waiting and a knight, who are conducting a forbidden love affair. They have enlisted the support of a guard, whose role is to warn them of the approach of dawn, when the knight will have to flee the lady-in-waiting's chamber in order to avoid detection.

"Thunder Only Happens"

This title is a partial quote of a line from the Fleetwood Mac song, "Dreams", written by Stevie Nicks.